Tempest In A Teapot

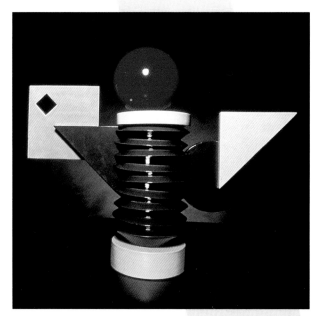

The Ceramic Art of Peter Shire

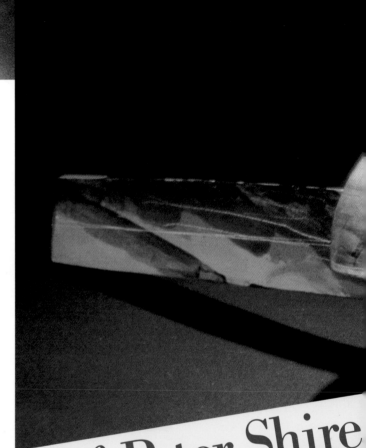

The Ceramic Art of Peter Shire

Tempest In
A Teapot

RIZZOLI
NEW YORK

For Henry Shire,
my father, and
Ava, my daughter.

First published in the
United States of America in
1991 by Rizzoli International
Publications, Inc.
300 Park Avenue South,
New York, NY 10010

Library of Congress
Cataloging-in-Publication Data
Drohojowska, Hunter, 1952-
Tempest in a teapot: the
ceramic art of Peter Shire:
essays / by Hunter Drohojowska
and Norman M. Klein;
foreword by Ettore Sottsass.
p.   cm.
Includes bibliographical
references.
ISBN 0-8478-1322-3
1. Shire, Peter—Criticism and
interpretation.   2. Ceramic
teapots—California—
History—20th century.
I. Klein, Norman M., 1945-
II. Title.
NK4210.S534D76   1991
90-48657
738′.092—dc20   CIP

Designed by Carlo Barile
Design associate:
Catrine Turillon
Design assistant: Mindy Ball
Set in type by
Graphic Arts Composition,
Philadelphia, Pennsylvania
Printed in Singapore

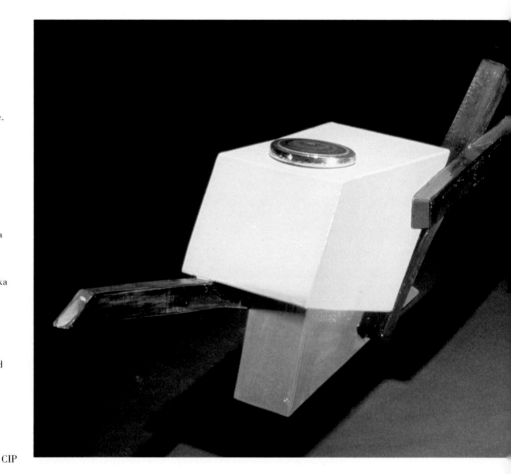

Cover photograph:
Jazz Modern, 1979
8 × 14½ × 4¾ in.

Page 1:
Stacked Donut, 1984
21 in. high

Frontispiece, left:
Picture Postcard, 1975
8½ × 20½ × 9⅜ in.

Frontispiece, right:
Teapot Bill Balance, 1975
7½ × 14 × 16 in.

Above:
Side Two, 1975
7 in. high

Opposite, left:
Auffen Gile Set, 1974
7½ × 10 × 6 in.

Opposite, right:
Hair Pot, 1975
9 in. high

Contents

Acknowledgments

I would like to thank: Mom—no explanation necessary; Donna, my wife—no explanation necessary; Anthony Scaccia—my high-school ceramics teacher who started it all; Terry Tokuda—the guy who was really there for me when it really counted; Waynna Kato—her help is appreciated; Didier La Caze—who brought a sense of the French charm into the studio; Cosmo Padilla—his skill helped bring it all to another level; Billy, my brother—no explanation possible; Leonard Koren—an intense connection confused by California Zen; Ettore Sottsass—who believed in me when no one as important as he did; Aldo Cibic, Michele DeLucchi, Matteo Thun, Marco Zanini—my support in Italy; Hunter Drohojowska—telepathy; Norman Klein—the whole Caballa wax; Jack Kling—who started me off on the right foot at Chouinard Institute; Jim Watterson—ceramics is the plane we met on and expanded; Jan Turner—for giving me my first show; Ken Brecher—who continues to be an inspiration; My collectors—where would I be without them?; Robert Janjigian and Daniel Waterman of Rizzoli International; and Carlo Barile—the designer of this "tome" who has done his best to bring New York elegance to this California chaos.

Peter Shire

Opposite:
Hemisphere, 1973-74
$4\frac{1}{2} \times 13 \times 6$ in.

Above:
Gile Kilns Set, 1974
$8 \times 8 \times 9$ in.

Left:
Hemisphere, 1975
$4\frac{1}{2}$ in. high

Above:
Taxco, 1976
7 in. high

Right:
Untitled, 1976
7¼ in. high

Following pages:
Top left:
Potemkin, 1977
12 × 11 × 31 in.

Bottom left:
Potemkin, 1977
10 × 10 × 28 in.

Top right:
Potemkin, 1977
11 × 10 × 30 in.

Bottom right:
Peach Pot and Cups,
1978
9 × 8 × 3½ in.

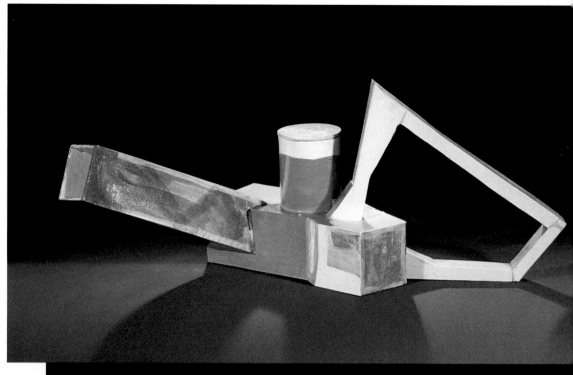

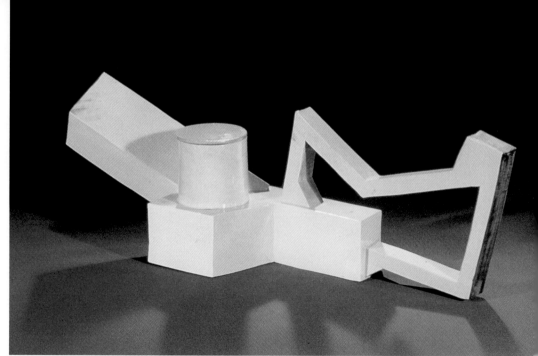

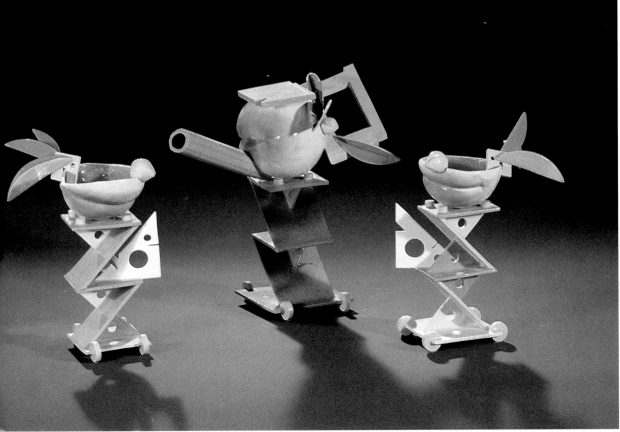

Left:
Taxco Teapot, 1977
Gouache on paper
22 × 30 in.

Above:
Bulbous Rupus, 1979
8½ in. high

Opposite:
Guitar, 1979
Gouache on paper
8 × 10 in.

Opposite:
Taxco Plume, 1978
9⅜ × 16½ × 8¾ in.

Above:
Henry Shire.
Scratchboard portrait of
Peter Shire for exhibition
notice, 1977

Foreword

A bout the year 1978–79 there was a magazine in L.A. called *WET*, and it was a very beautiful Californian magazine, dealing with soap, water, bathing suits, naked bodies, hot springs, and these kinds of things.

One day in that magazine I saw a picture of a ceramic teapot, and I just about fell off my chair. Those ceramics were so new, so right-for-the-moment, so fresh, so witty, and so full of information for the future that I said to myself: "I need to meet the gentleman who did these things."

The gentleman's name was Peter Shire.

I don't know what happened later, but one very sunny day, in a sort of a happy L.A. suburb, with hills, trees, lakes, etc., I met Peter Shire in his studio, and he had a black beard, shiny eyes, strange bermuda shorts, black hairy legs, and he was in a permanent state of humor. His ceramics were a sort of collage, a sort of unstable collage of more or less broken geometric volumes, more or less broken mathematical surfaces, and then there were lines crossing everything and there were memories on top. Most of the time the memories were of pale Californian colors and landscapes, maybe of beaches, or of sundaes, or maybe of Sundays, with candy-girls skating all around. But Peter was not only using Californian broken memories; he was putting together every piece of cultural information he could collect from everywhere, and every smallest leftover of memories, from the East, or from the West, that may have landed on the California shore.

Even the technique to me was very new. He wasn't working the ceramic on the wheel and he wasn't putting the ceramic together with his hands like a sculptor, but he was producing ceramic planes and glueing them together

Opposite:
Cover of <u>WET: The Magazine of Gourmet Bathing</u> (Venice, California), February/March 1977. Ettore Sottsass first saw Shire's work in <u>WET</u>

Above:
Peter Shire. <u>Untitled</u>, 1976
7¼ in. high

like you would build a house of cards. And then he was glueing together other elements like strings or cylinders or cubes or handles—spouts, cups, and everything.

To me it was like looking at a fantastic acrobat able to do movements and combinations of movements, and to produce figures that nobody could produce, ever: to me it was like sitting in a nice chair and looking at somebody who, not showing any pain, not showing any aggressivity, and without me even noticing, could destroy in a fraction of a second, a whole cultural system, a whole traditional, balanced, cultural logic. Then in a fraction of a second, without me noticing again, could recompose all the pieces in a totally unexpected new logic system, into which I am immediately taken and swallowed.

I know that there is always a new logic to be found which connects old broken logics together, because things are always changing: changing dimension, weight, color, distance, speed, etc. And I also knew that the Peter Shire new logic was always a very possible one, one that was nicely working, that could be the right one to understand or at least to help you walk among the many mysteries that are inhabiting our days and nights.

That afternoon I went into Peter Shire's studio, it was a nice day. We became friends and went to have lunch in Chinatown, at the Hunan restaurant, Imperial cuisine, very good restaurant. And now that I am writing, many years have passed, maybe ten, and during these many years together with other friends, we went through that strange event called Memphis; we passed all these years designing furniture and objects and architectures, and Peter was being interviewed and published on many magazine covers, like a star, and he was working a lot, and now he is a sculptor, he is doing big sculptures, as big as he can, and he is becoming more and more Californian and looking for new logical systems, for new combinations, new figures, new standards to rebuild and put together the broken pieces (left on the floor) of the life which every day, every, every day is going to be destroyed.

But it is a long time since we have had lunch together at the Hunan restaurant.

Ettore Sottsass

ETTORE SOTTSASS is principal of Sottsass Associati, Milan, an architecture and design firm. His influence on late-twentieth-century design has been remarkable, especially through his design work for Olivetti and his association with Alchymia and Memphis, design movements in which he played a founding role.

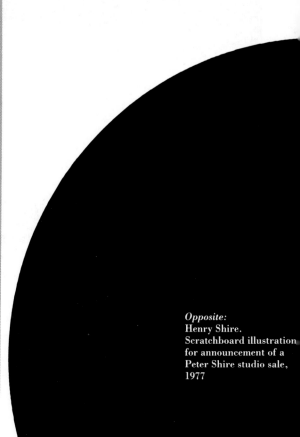

Opposite:
Henry Shire.
Scratchboard illustration
for announcement of a
Peter Shire studio sale,
1977

Tempest in a Teapot:

The Social History of

In "*Ode on a Grecian Urn*," Keats compares ceramics to the "still unravished bride of quietness." She "cannot fade," as "beauty is truth, truth beauty." Peter Shire's ceramics is much less fixed than that; it concentrates more on what has "faded," and what has been "ravished"—more like the bride "stripped bare" in Duchamp's *Large Glass* than the bride in Keats's Grecian urn.

For Shire, the medium of ceramics is certainly not a fixed pedestal art; nor is it exclusively industrial product design; nor again is it the simple craft of the "homely" potter. Rather, it engages all three at once.

Together, they force a volatility into ceramics. This may sound odd at first, speaking of ceramics as volatile, but let us presume for the moment that the humble teapot belongs to a very changeable tradition, utterly dependent on the intricacies of consumer marketing, and see where this assumption leads us.

In 1974, Shire began working on a series of architectonic teapots, using references to steel constructions and modern architecture, but in the fragile medium of ceramics. New glazes that fired at a much lower temperature allowed him to play more easily with random shapes, and "designer" colors, and to make references to many media within the same piece. As so much has been said about these works' whimsically subversive quality, we can examine them more in terms of social history.

That would suggest a different range of questions. For example, what do these teapots "say" about the role of the applied artist/designer in the history of modernism? How do we find the same "statements" in art nouveau stoneware, or Bauhaus functionalism? At first glance, Shire's teapots seem only to contain short quotations out of context, hardly an undiluted version of form following function—if anything, quite the reverse. They seem to cross-fertilize a Googie luncheonette miniature with Tatlin's Tower, or a Marianne Brandt teapot.

Some modernist strategies inform the work directly, futurist dynamism in particular: the teapots look as if they are about to break apart, but are held in freeze-frame for posterity. The machine aesthetic takes a header.

Myths of the ceramic arts are still contained in these teapots, or rather held in suspension: the "homely" potter meets the upscale industrial designer and the fine artist. Let us take the problems one at a time, and imagine a history for each. They are designed to be fictions, so we should answer them with fictions.

Opposite:
Henry Shire.
Scratchboard study for a
Peter Shire exhibition
announcement, The
Homey Potter, 1980

Peter Shire's Ceramics

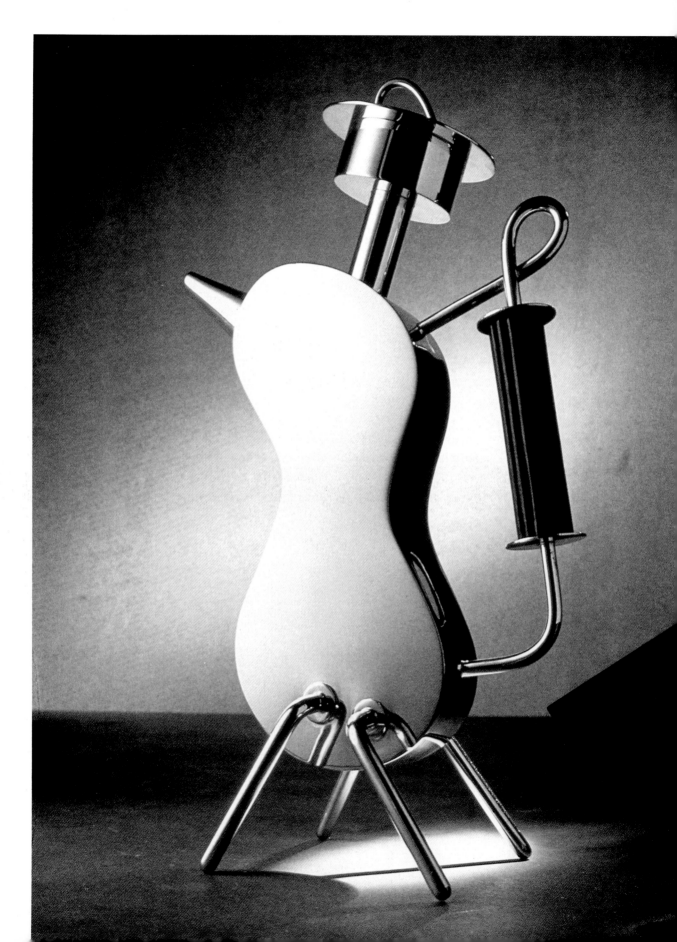

Above:
Marianne Brandt
Teapot, 1924
Brass and ebony

Opposite:
Peter Shire. Giotto, 1989
Silver and ebony
15½ in. high

I. Teapots As Household Interiors

In the middle thirties, German critic Walter Benjamin ruminated about the furnishings of the early-twentieth-century apartment. He was fascinated by the use of ornament in interiors, particularly in objects made by the Belgian designer Henry Van de Velde: "It represents art's last attempt to escape from its ivory tower, which is besieged by technology. Art nouveau mobilizes all the reserves of inwardness. They find their expression in the mediumistic line-language in the flower as the symbol of naked, vegetal nature confronting a technically armed environment."

Benjamin goes on to describe the fiction that is created within the apartment, as if the furnishings worked like a short story without characters, only clues. The clues can be found in chairs, pottery, pictures—fragments of how the occupant views history, travel, the world of work. This becomes the introspective "world theater" of the private individual. Inside the home, an inwardness is layered behind drapery, settees, inside cabinets—to push the crisis of work and industrial culture away. Like a detective novel, the occupant leaves a trail of household objects, in the kitchen and the sitting room, on shelves, in drawers, pointing toward imaginary crimes that give the usefulness of everyday objects a mystery they ordinarily would not have.

Benjamin sees a fantasy narrative within the interior decoration of private life. What's more, he sees this story as uneven, about corruption, childlike dreams of overcoming evil—exotic adventure in your own living room.

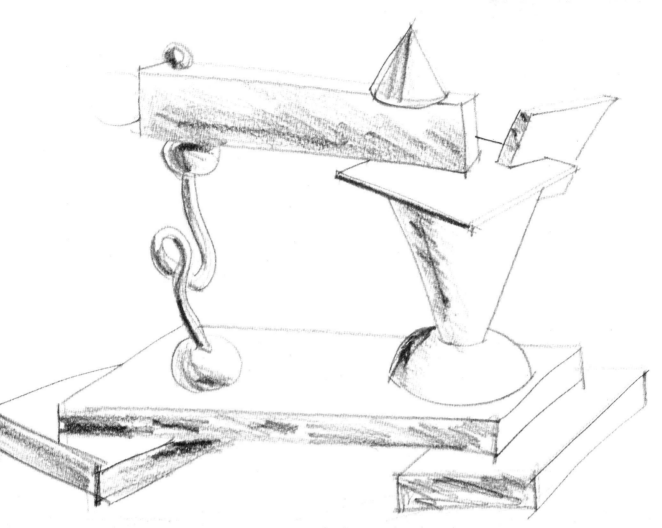

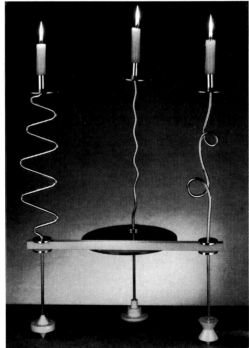

Above:
Peter Shire. <u>Study for
Viennese Coffee Pot</u>, 1983
Pencil on paper
9 × 7⅜ in.

Right:
Peter Shire. <u>Tre Steli</u>,
1989
Chromed metal
15 × 9 × 21 in.

He shows us a besieged early consumer, in a world not yet providing the services or objects for personal reverie we see today. (Obviously, television markets this "inwardness" for us now.) By our standards, the world at the turn of the twentieth century was still rather primitive; its consumer industries were still not marketed electronically. Not even its consumer objects were made in huge factories as we understand them today. But the conflict of objects brought on by consumerism had begun—the struggle to turn housewares into industrial statements. (We already see the first "industrial" kitchens: the flour hoosiers, the quirky apple peelers, and so on.)

In such an interior, pre-industrial forms begin to appear rather whimsical, as if the older ways had lost their purpose: porcelain gourds by Taxile Doat, with art nouveau reliefs climbing out of artificial shells. It is a secret shared by the applied artist and the consumer—a fiction one finds in the various arts-and-crafts institutes set up in Europe after 1890. In fact, English science fiction was, in many ways, invented by designers fantasizing a future based on nostalgia for the lost craftsman (George Macdonald and William Morris, for example). What was this secret? Many artisan crafts were endangered: print layout, wood-engraving, bookbinding, woodcarving (furniture also), pottery, and, of course, ceramics in general. And so were the workplace, the city, the home. A state of siege had emerged in the material culture of everyday life.

There was a ghost in the machine—or more a contradiction. Emblems of the lost artisan haunted the industrial process, phantom intersections of machines and gardens, often rather ghoulish or quirky. And we find these emblems in any number of media, cross references between machine production and rustic imagery (such as Mackintosh designing factory molds based on landscapes). It was a mixed message, almost a cynical joke, to see the emblems of landscape transformed into machine shapes—or to see household objects made to look like industrial vegetation.

For a half-century or more, that single problem seemed to obsess the applied arts in particular, even studio versions, from the German Werkbund to the Bauhaus, from the Morris Company to early moderne, and any number of independent craftsman along the way (and also, of course in virtually all the media where art nouveau designers worked). The products that came out were as eccentric as a Rube Goldberg cartoon, or early Dr. Seuss: electric fixtures designed like cathedral windows; living rooms paneled like medieval hunting lodges; intentionally rude pottery, with city scenes dropped inside, like industrial streets sinking into quicksand.

And with studio ceramics, to this day we find the same contradictions, in the grand tradition of the schizoid role of the applied artist: bowls as upside-down ladies' hats; candy dishes like chimeras with their heads missing. The list could run on for pages—and be exemplified, for our advanced consumer civilization, by Peter Shire's hyper-modernist collisions in miniature, held together under the humble category of the teapot.

For generations now, artists have known that this populist utopia was a bit ludicrous: to make believe that the independent craftsman can also be an industrial designer and a fine artist—and appease all three markets in the same piece. I say "make believe" because the results are so wonderfully self-conscious, so

intentionally driven by the cynical realities of marketing. They register more like a cynical conversation after hours than convinced formalism, however pundits may want to uplift ceramics and the applied arts. What makes them unique is more important than the need to defend them.

They are invaded art works, standing in for the invasion of private life. Markets are translated into imaginary armies fighting for recognition on the surface of a ceramic object— political appliqué in the decorative arts. What throws people is the site of this battle zone. It is not in art galleries or bohemias or at avant-garde rallies. Instead, the battle is centered around the private world of the consumer: the home, household objects, fantasy knick-knacks, crossover art/design items. As Benjamin explains, "The interior is the retreat of art."

The battle is displayed ironically, like a Greek vase about a siege in the bedroom: Lysistrata circling her warrior husband. The battle subverts the myth of the useful object, by making the useful very fragile—crystal machines, with streets or battleships sunk inside. It speaks to the consumer's memory directly, rather than through a museum discourse. It contains a modernity more akin to postmodernism than to modernism—and it has for a century at least.

These seemingly naive objects contain a rather complex art language, with a long tradition. Let us summarize a few of the traces one finds in teapots—their fictions—evident in art nouveau, and in the work of Peter Shire:

1. Their schizoid imagery: They suggest a lopsided consumer narrative, like random objects in a shopping bag mating on the way home. Shire's scorpions mate with plumbing parts and children's blocks. One senses these perverse morphologies in titles Shire assigns to his teapots (rather off-the-cuff): *Cubist Steam*, *Auffen Gile* (monkey sex), *Mexican Bauhaus* (referring to the architect Barragan). In art nouveau also, this miscegenation is very apparent in stoneware gourds invaded by painterly surfaces.

2. Their blend of the "rustic" with the industrial: These teapots comment on the invasion of privacy by factory products, either through an upside-down primitivism, or by outright appropriation of industrial shapes into the hand-crafted object.

3. The usefulness they subvert: These teapots announce the collisions between the applied arts and pedestal art. The teapot is essentially a vernacular object, a craft item for the home. Tip it over and pour it out. But once it is aestheticized, it becomes an art quiz on the meaning of "useful": Where's the spout? Doesn't it look like an ocean liner about to set out to sea? Clearly, the designer teapot is made in a small shop—by the "homely" potter. However, at the same time, it can be mass-produced, according to a prototype made by the industrial designer. And finally, it can be set on a pedestal in an art gallery. Still, isn't there a preliminary moment when we ask: Could I actually pour from this? Three personae make war within the same object, in different combinations, according to the artist's strategy in the given piece.

4. Asymmetrical elements added to complicate how the eye sees the dimensions of the object: Shire, for example, began his teapots in 1974 with one strategy that sounds very modest on first hearing—he wanted to make them three-dimensional. Teapots are usually seen as two-dimensional lines complicated by volume, still a very reduced syntax. By contrast, Shire wanted the eye to stall often along the way and not find a single way to see. He

Right:
Peter Shire.
Announcement for a Peter
Shire exhibition at Janus
Gallery, 1975

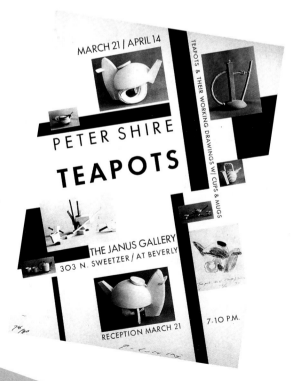

wanted to stop the viewer, much as collage might, or sculpture, or montage. He wanted an asymmetrical map of possibilities, based on an odd variety of sources (Calder, futurism, collapsed inner cities, constructivism, uneven versions of functionalism, allegorical abstraction). That suggests a valuable warning for studying teapots, but also for all the studio and applied arts. We should not concentrate on their timeless beauty—their balance and symmetry, as in Keats's Grecian urn. When we do, it erases their cues to a larger world. In addition to studying technique, and the harmony of glaze, one should ask: How does the mix of opposites announce the roles of the artist, the fantasies of the consumer, the pressures of the market?

II. Living Rooms Decorated Like Bridges

By the 1920s, very little of the handcrafted was available to buy; the industrial invasion had taken over the home, from electricity to kitchen appliances. Industrial products had now replaced the handmade consumer object in virtually every key market. As a result, the applied arts merged into industrial design.

As in the metalwork of Marianne Brandt, a particular favorite of Shire's, teapots by the twenties rarely commented on the rude forms of the lost craftsman, or the lost landscape (as in art nouveau's ironic use of vegetation). They were now much more "approving" of industry: the craftsman as industrial designer (making use of the brass and steel of the factory) had fully emerged.

Modernist objects, whether abstract or streamlined, are as pluralistic as art nouveau

Opposite:
Peter Shire. Study for Cubist Steam, 1978
Ink on paper
8½ × 11 in.

Top, inset:
Alexander Calder. Flying Colors, 1973
Aerospace paint on a Braniff jetliner

Bottom, inset
Alexander Calder. A Universe, 1934
Motor-driven mobile: painted iron pipe, wire, and wood with string
40½ in. high

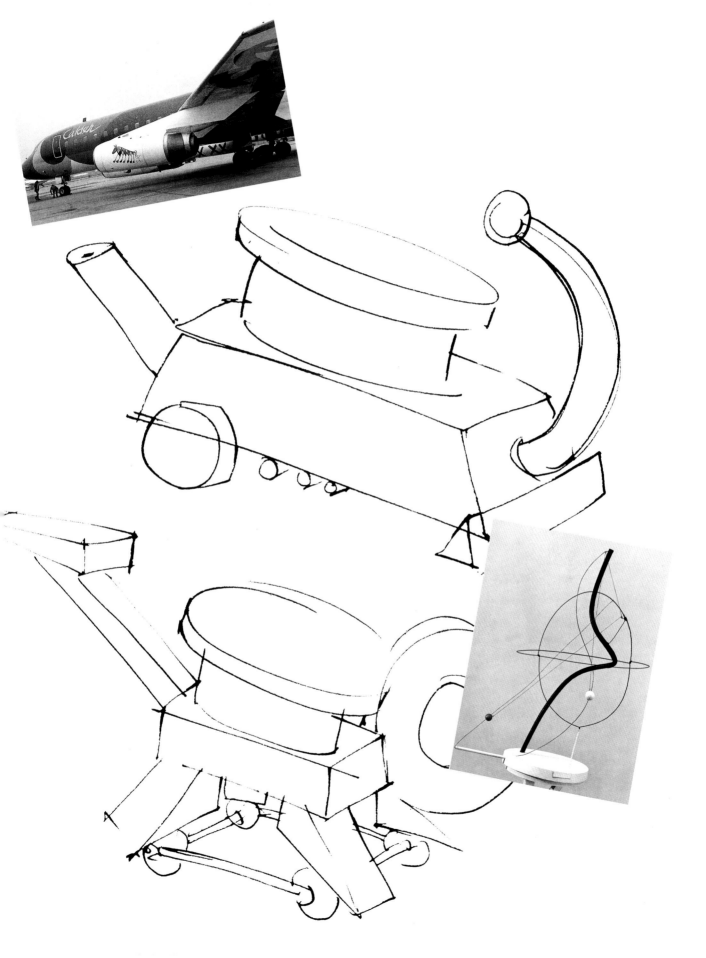

SHIRE
8-25-1985

Opposite:
**Peter Shire. Bel-Air
Chair, 1981**
45½ × 43½ × 49 in.
(Memphis production)

Above:
**Peter Shire. Bel-Air Chair
Teapot, 1985**
Gouache on paper
10 × 14 in.

Above:
Peter Shire. Anchorage,
1982
16 in. high
(Memphis production)

Right:
Peter Shire. Big Sur, 1986
75 in. long
(Memphis production)

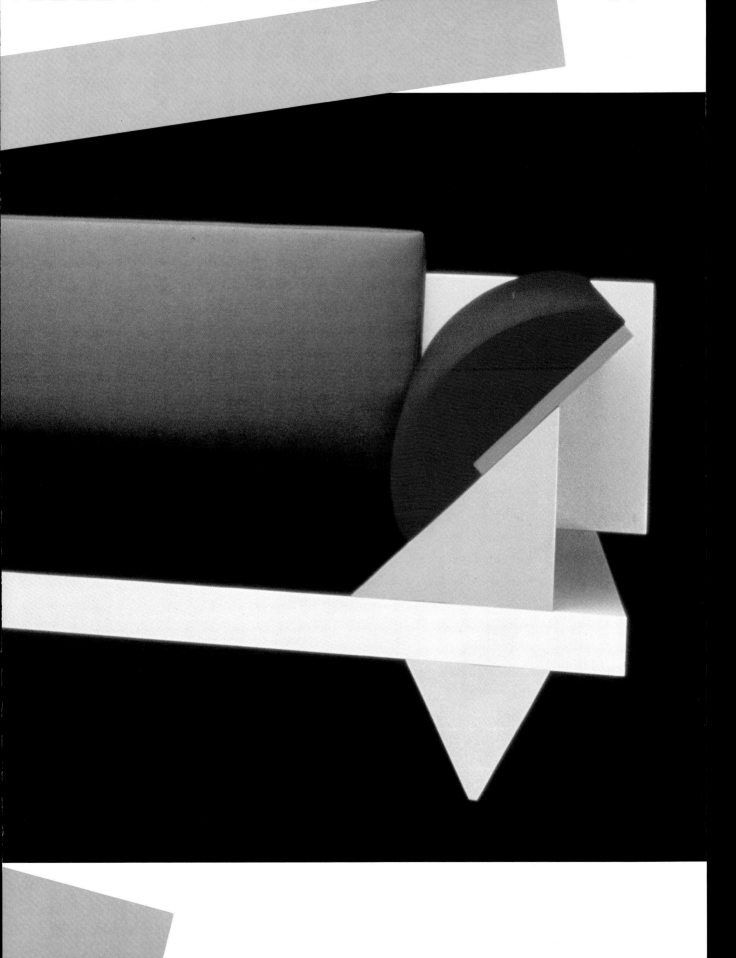

pieces in many ways. They are often more about packaging than truth to materials.

The odd futurist ceramics that Shire finds very compelling are pluralistic; they are metaphysical ironies, circus gags about machine dynamism, militaristic nostalgia of the Mussolini era. The same is true of the ironies he sees in Bauhaus versions of household furnishings, a very important source for his work. The modernist designer subverted three-dimensionality as much as the painter subverted perspective. Form collapses function. Shire admired Loewy's designs, but not for the reasons one might assume. He saw them as glamorous camouflage, as "shrouds" that *covered* the machine parts—more like form follows market fantasy, in order to hide function—as consumer memories ripe for restatement.

III. Ceramic Freeways

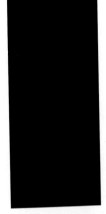

Shire's work operates within the tradition of crossover, a kind of modernist pluralism that began in the middle nineteenth century, if not earlier. It records whimsically how packaging of all sorts developed. In Shire's teapots, industrial shapes subvert the operations of the handmade object, much the way downtown Los Angeles invaded the older wooden housing around it.

Opposite:
Henry Shire. Ceramic Freeways, 1982
Scratchboard
9¾ × 13⅜ in.

From within a mile of Shire's studio, virtually from his back window at home, one can see the lost possibilities of the functionalist dream. High-rise bank buildings hover like smog above vanishing communities. As one critic has said, downtown Los Angeles is the city of the future fifteen years too late.

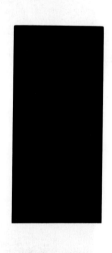

Just east of the Echo Park district of Los Angeles where Shire grew up (and still lives),

William Reagh has been photographing the changing Los Angeles landscape since the 1950s. His work is an important inspiration to Shire for the way in which that landscape impacts on his work. "Los Angeles and its interaction with my work is inevitable. It's a funny, driving part of what I do. My work is not representational, yet it arises from a desire to create one's own world because the world of Los Angeles and its development is so weird and rapacious, on a very capricious level, and it manifests itself in my work."

Above:
William Reagh. Los Angeles, 3rd and Hill Streets, 1955

Opposite:
Top:
William Reagh. Los Angeles, 3rd and Hill Streets, 1973

Bottom:
William Reagh. Los Angeles, 3rd and Hill Streets, 1986

Following pages:
Top left:
William Reagh. Los Angeles, 5th Street looking toward downtown, 1959

Bottom left:
William Reagh. Los Angeles, 5th Street looking toward downtown, 1983

Top right:
William Reagh. Los Angeles, view east toward the 3rd Street Tunnel and Bunker Hill, 1963

Bottom right:
William Reagh. Los Angeles, view east toward the 3rd Street Tunnel and Bunker Hill, 1986

the bulldozing of old neighborhoods competed with the sudden appearance of a vertical downtown—an alien presence in an embankment of emptied lots. This cataclysmically uneven city has influenced the inverse modernity we find in his work, a whimsical mixture of craft and machine aesthetic.

He studied at the old Chouinard Institute, in a very mixed program: functionalist design, minimalist modernism, and basic draftsmanship. This, along with the years he worked alongside his father—a formally trained artist turned carpenter—gave him a mixed sense of how art products should be made as well. He could lay Formica professionally, work ceramics with the eye of a potter, and was presumably going to become a modernist designer: "After the oil embargo, I sold my '56 Ford pickup, before the gas hikes made it too expensive to drive. I spent the money to rebrick an old kiln—to start doing porcelain. Very soon, I realized I didn't want to do porcelain at all. I was making earthenware. While bricking my cone 10 kiln, the bricklayer kept telling me, 'You better work hard to pay for all this.' Ironically, at the time, I was working on the *Aufen Gile* teapots, which completely changed my direction."

Right:
Henry Shire.
Scratchboard illustration
for announcement of a
Peter Shire exhibition at
the Janus Gallery, 1981

HENRY SHIRE

Left:
Peter Shire. <u>Gile Kilns
Set</u>, 1974
$8 \times 8 \times 9$ in.

Below:
Peter Shire. <u>Auffen Gile
Set</u>, 1974
$7\frac{1}{2} \times 10 \times 6$ in.

Following pages:
Left:
Peter Shire's studio, 1983

Right:
Peter Shire in his studio,
1983

His style took a turn with two pieces in particular from 1974; one he calls *Gile Kilns*, the other *Auffen Gile*. They involve simple shapes in a collapsing format, difficult to photograph because of the many angles and shadows they hold, and the differences when one shifts point of view. They are reminders of a Malevich suprematist drawing coming unglued, though in a range of soft, almost sunbleached, California colors.

Above all, he had wanted to introduce the sculptural into teapots, to rearrange the exterior volume. He was influenced in part by a Bauhaus show at the Pasadena Art Museum in 1968-69. The metal teapots of Marianne Brandt struck him, in their surprising contrast of round belly (for the teapot) and industrial angles.

The teapots also reminded him of piles of wood scraps he used to see on his father's work sites, and that they always struck him as very beautiful, as records of work done, as distinct from the building itself—of the craftsman. The retrospective sense of these woodpiles is very important to him—"what's left after it's happened." He compares them to "a constructivist composition where the artist is absent."

Shire still refers to his subject as "the act of work," and the pieces as resisting, "on the edge." It was important to eliminate the act of throwing a pot within the piece, except for the lid.

After this series was completed, as Shire began to locate his areas more clearly, these applications of the sculptural and industrial imitation were expanded. But at the center was still the crisis of the crafted object, the notion that construction was an emblem for

work. To play with an uncertainty he saw in industrial design, he continued to add more "flying parts," and "levitational" elements, and to tease out the notion of the machine object as breakable ceramic—a contradiction in use. He explains: "Often industrial design gives us a better world whether we want it or not."

By 1979, Shire had begun to link up with international architects, and with the Memphis movement from Milan. However, his point of arrival followed the general problem presented here—that of an alternative tradition that is very much engaged to social experience, a wide blend of markets, and the language of consumer culture.

His teapots are a commentary as well on the confusion of art practice (functionalism meets consumer design, under the wing of modernism), and on the need for a regenerative sense of work outside of the formal art world. He remains on something of a hairline crack, between high design and the dream of the populist craftsman, while regularly showing in galleries. And he feels that the tradition behind his work must be infinitely older than art nouveau, though the events of the late nineteenth century add a crisis to consumer experience that is uniquely important. It is clear that the contradiction gives spirit and surprise to his work, particularly in the 1990s, as the American economy cracks like a teapot, and new strategies are needed to convey these issues in the arts.

"My work has always been designed for people to have, in their house. The other parts are not as important. Hopefully, the skeleton will reveal the beast."

Norman M. Klein

NORMAN M. KLEIN is a Los Angeles-based critic and historian of the arts, media, and mass culture. He is the author of several books, including *Twentieth-Century Art Theory*.

The Playground

f Modern Desire

Peter Shire's favorite movie is *Playtime*. In Jacques Tati's mordantly funny critique of late-sixties, hyper-modernized Paris, unwitting citizens find themselves constantly victimized by the objects and institutions of their postwar leisure-time lives. The props are the true characters of this tale, subversive of the best intentions: a trash can disguised as a marble column and advertised with the slogan "Thro-out Greek style"; an urn-shaped lamp that dispenses cigarettes when the shade is pulled upward; restaurant chairs adorned with wicked, crown-shaped ornaments that tear clothing and impale hurried waiters. Ugly and foolish though this furniture appears, it is embraced and admired by the film's Parisians, who view it as symbolic of their newly industrialized, Americanized suc-

Left:
Jacques Tati. Film still from
Playtime

cess. Paris's traditional monuments—the Eiffel Tower, for instance—are only observed when reflected in the thick modern glass of an opening office door.

That Shire would admire this not-so-fictional film is easy to see. The subtext of *Playtime* is the subversive power of style. With abundant humor, the collision of modernism's ideals against the desires of the real world are made suddenly clear—an obvious theme in Shire's work.

Today, Shire is known for his wide-ranging designs for furniture, jewelry, fashion accessories, architecture, stagesets—even a disco for the 1984 Olympics—and his ongoing relationship with the Memphis movement. All recombine the shapes and colors he terms "Cookie Cutter Moderne." However, this essay focuses on his primary interest: ceramics.

Like so many artists of his generation, Shire has been dodging, upsetting, or confronting the legacies of modernism since 1974, the date he affixes to his first mature work, *Auffen Gile*, a ceramic teapot with a box-shaped white body surrounded by a storm of multi-hued, constructivist-inspired beams that form the handle, spout, and base.

Shire chose ceramics from the pantheon of late-twentieth-century art media in part *because* of its problematic status. There was, in the late sixties the much-discussed if futile battle of art versus craft, as well as the more complex philosophical dismantling of the modernist heritage. Shire was the beneficiary of two decades of exploration and experimentation, of sculpture in an expanded field, and of the erosion of the historical art posture, which had maintained oil painting at the apex of the marketing pyramid.

He contributes to a uniquely southern California art history where ceramics comprise a

Jacques Tati is one of Shire's favorite filmmakers, and Playtime,
perhaps more than any other Tati film, embodies the "man
versus machine theme" that so intrigues Shire. "Playtime
represents the machine gone amuck, the machine that was to have
solved all of our problems, but which made more of them instead.
It portrays a funny dream-world, where you got everything you
wanted, but lost all that you had.

reaction to and refutation of the modernist
separation of fine and applied arts. With his
characteristically wry humor, Shire explains,
"I love art and I love clay, and I wasn't going
to give up one for the other. It's like, 'My wife
is ugly but I'm bringing her anyway.'"

Critic Christopher Knight has written inci-
sively about the impact of the ceramics movement at the Otis Art Institute (now Otis/Par-
sons) in the late 1950s. It was there, he points
out, that Peter Voulkos and his students John
Mason and Ken Price created an authentic
revolution in ceramics that had less to do with
the abstract expressionist heritage than with a
break with Western traditions of pottery. Instead of adhering to the ceramist's ideal of
seamless harmony between surface and form,
they turned the two elements against one another. As an example, he cites Voulkos's *Vase
with Two Handles* (1951), in which a "fluid
delicate white and pale celadon glaze . . .
runs and drips and puddles across the irregu-
lar surface." He also mentions the bulbous

early cups of Price, which are glazed with "playfully familiar, two-dimensional emblems," such as a brightly colored chevron.

Knight writes: "In pitting muscularity of form against fragility of surface, or idiosyncratic three-dimensional form against familiar two-dimensional shape, Voulkos and Price achieve works whose internal elements compete with one another for our attention; they assume an ambiguous life and personality all their own."[1]

These ideas were spawned by the modernist traditions of fine art and applied to ceramics. Voulkos, Mason, Price—as well as Billy Al Bengston, who worked in ceramics at that time—and their peers and followers did not think of themselves as potters, but conceptualized and executed their work as artists.

Shire was fully cognizant of these developments as a student at the Chouinard Art Institute in the late sixties. (He graduated in 1970.) He remembers Price as one of the greatest influences on his work. He recalls

Left:
Jacques Tati. Film still from
Playtime. A "modern"
ceiling descends upon guests
at a nightclub

Price's snail-handled cups, exhibited at the Riko Mizuno Gallery in 1969: "I saw ceramics could be stuff you could love rather than big lumps of clay trying to take the art world on its own terms. That stuff was playing into the business that sculpture has to be heroic and macho. Price wasn't doing any of that."

What Price did was to challenge the prevailing postwar American association of significance and scale, especially with regard to the use of ceramics as a major sculptural medium. His work is deliberately "unsignificant," relying on humorous references to popular culture to undermine the pretensions that had come to be associated with Abstract Expressionism.

In Shire's teapots, the contradictions of form and surface conflate the visual vocabularies of various movements in twentieth-century art history. A constructivist teapot's angular forms may be further fractured by a cubist glazing technique so that Cezanne and Malevich meet in the same humble vessel. Or the surfaces of the same sort of constructivist form may be glazed in the optically-charged, orphic color combinations of Robert Delaunay, or in the splatter and drip manner of Jackson Pollock, or in the swirling and checkerboard combinations of op art.

Such appropriation is a subversive strategy underscored by the use of ceramics. The high ideals of modernist enterprise—not the least being "form follows function"—are persistently undermined. A teapot may be the central prop in a dialogue between two people, but Shire's teapots contain a dialogue between art historical perspectives.

Often this is a droll conversation, but it is never a superficial one. Shire likes to challenge preconceptions, but he is neither being ironic nor questioning the validity of modern art practice. His puns are sly, we think, as we ponder the skeins and splashes of Pollock's *Autumn Rhythm* reduced to the less heroic surface of a teapot. We pause to wonder about the utopian visions of the constructivists, now captured in a series of architectural teapots that Shire has irreverently labeled *Mexican Bauhaus*.

The subversive, decentered nature of ceramics gave Shire permission to root around in the modernist lexicon and borrow whatever his heart and mind desired. Shire found comfort in this method of making art without joining the club, in the ability of staying on the fringe of the gallery-museum-critic nexus. "One of my real approaches is that of reaction. I tend to do that. Some of my best pieces make fun of pretensions."

For Shire, the field of ceramics—because of the implied issues of utility and domesticity—constitutes a symbolic blackboard on which the formulae of life and art may be continually redrawn. In a neutral context, it might be difficult to see how large a role biography plays in Shire's oeuvre. But, in addition to art history, his ceramics are inspired by the landscape of his life—the neighborhood of Echo Park where he was born and raised, and where, at age forty-two, he lives with his wife Donna and daughter Ava.

It is difficult to overstate the impact of environment and family on Shire's ceramics. If he chose the medium in part because of its critical position, it is also because the vessels are inherently symbolic of home and the interior life. The colors, marks, and shapes of his teapots are also echoes of the barrio: gang graffiti, hot metal-flake paint jobs on the cars of local lowriders, the pastel stucco of the boxy architecture, the lusty Third World exoticism of Cuban sandwiches and passion fruit liquados, and evening paseos around Echo Park Lake. Echo Park, one of the last pockets of lazy, old L.A., is a vestigial reminder of a slow, Mediterranean sort of life that has been largely developed out of existence in the rush to create a "world-class city."

Shire's parents, Henry and Barbara, were both supporters of the labor movement and settled in Echo Park in part because it was a center for left-wing political activity. Shire remembers being one of three white Jewish boys at Belmont High; it was an adolescence that prepared him for his ongoing sense of being an outsider. He claims this was yet another reason to major in ceramics, to be an outcast from the continuum of fine-art practice.

Shire's connection to Echo Park was reinforced by his mother's store, The Soap Plant, which opened on Sanborn Junction in 1971. Now run by Peter's younger brother Billy, the store has become a successful boutique at its new location on Melrose Avenue. But early in Peter's career, the Echo Park store was an outlet for his first ceramics.

Shire's father was a trained artist, but the Depression had forced him into the occupation of carpentry. Both Shire's grandfathers were similarly employed—his paternal grandfather was a cabinetmaker trained in an English guild; his maternal grandfather designed furniture for the family firm in San Francisco.

As a boy, Peter helped his father build

cabinets and furniture, skills the artist would use in his ceramic work and, ultimately, in his furniture and sculpture. His teapots are not thrown or carved or coiled from clay. Instead, squarish slabs of semi-hardened clay are joined at the seams like so many pieces of plywood. They are literally "built," a technique that contributes to their architectural appearance.

In this discussion of "ceramics," there remains one question: Why teapots? Shire has concentrated his efforts on this one species of vessel, only occasionally in conjunction with cups and never with saucers.

First of all, there is the issue of function. Shire calls the teapot "the Holy Grail of pottery," meaning it is one of the most complex and difficult exercises in clay. The joining of dissimilar elements, the issue of balance relative to the placement of the handle and spout, the fact that the teapot actually must pour tea without spilling or dripping, combine to make it a technical challenge. While Shire attaches outlandish appendages, whirls of beams and tubes that surround the body, the teapot will pour.

If it did not function, it would be a less radical statement, a defeat by those who would wedge ceramics into the realm of sculp-

Above:
Peter Shire in his studio, 1983

ture. "That battle had been won by Mason and Arneson. After them, half of what you would see as ceramic sculpture would be little mountain effigies," explains Shire. "The material is so dominant it's almost pointless to do it."

Instead of underscoring the plasticity of clay, Shire dedicates considerable effort to disguising it, even though it might contain a hot brew of Earl Grey. Thus utility is admitted and subverted simultaneously. The teapots are often so complicated that it is daunting to pick them up. "I eliminate references to the hand, to the small, discreet, and comfortable object. I began by making them confrontational so you'd have a hard time grabbing them," he confessed. "They had to be more than groovy little constructions."

Apart from form and function, there is the matter of sexuality. According to Chinese

symbology, the opening covered by the lid may represent the female principle, while the phallic spout clearly indicates the male. Both are inherent in any teapot—a continuation of the dialogue—and many of Shire's teapots are subtle metaphors for intercourse and sensual involvement. Juxtapositions of erect cones or pillars with voluptuous spheres and dishes, the nestled, suggestive fit of recurring shapes, and the juicy surfaces and colors offer abundant evidence.

Finally, the ritual of tea—with its implication of high society and formalized behavior—is something Shire wanted to upset via the influence of Lewis Carroll. "It was a way to handle problems I have with ideas of elegance and perfection, things that I love and hate at the same time," he says. "It was like my choice of pastel colors. I was so revolted by them, I had to use them. It's part of the artist's urge to make it your own, to reshape the world. And objects can make you happy. They are not of themselves important. But, I think Robert Henri said, art is the signpost on the road that leads you back into yourself, to your place in the universe."

Shire admits it comes back to family, too, to the working class sympathies inherited from his parents. The functional aspect of the teapot relieves some of the elitism inevitably associated with the arena of fine art.

"I never drink tea," he says. "But I think it's a good omen if I work on something that I don't actually do. There is an aspect to my work that depends on a life that I longed for, not one that I had."

Hunter Drohojowska

HUNTER DROHOJOWSKA is Chair, Department of Liberal Arts and Sciences, The Otis Art Institute/Parsons School of Design, Los Angeles. She is at work on a biography of Georgia O'Keeffe.

Opposite, top:
Fleetline Vogue, 1979
6¼ × 14½ × 3½ in.

Opposite, bottom:
Fleetline, 1979
7 in. high

Above:
Peter Shire in
his studio, 1983

1. Knight, Christopher. "Otis Clay: A Revolution in the Tradition of Pottery," Los Angeles Herald Examiner, September 29, 1982: C3.

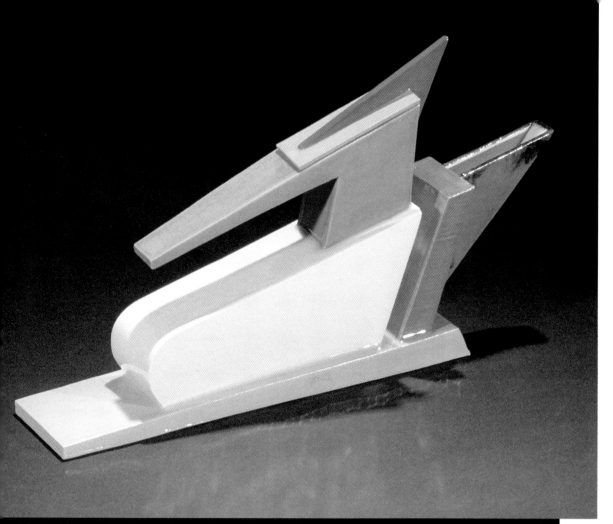

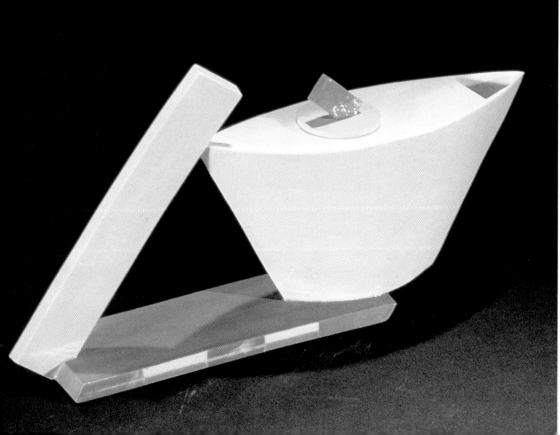

Right:
Jazz Modern, 1979
$8 \times 14\frac{1}{2} \times 4\frac{3}{4}$ in.

Above:
Mexican Bauhaus
Bookend, 1980
7 in. high

Right:
Mexican Bauhaus, 1980
$8\frac{1}{2} \times 15\frac{7}{8} \times 9\frac{3}{4}$ in.

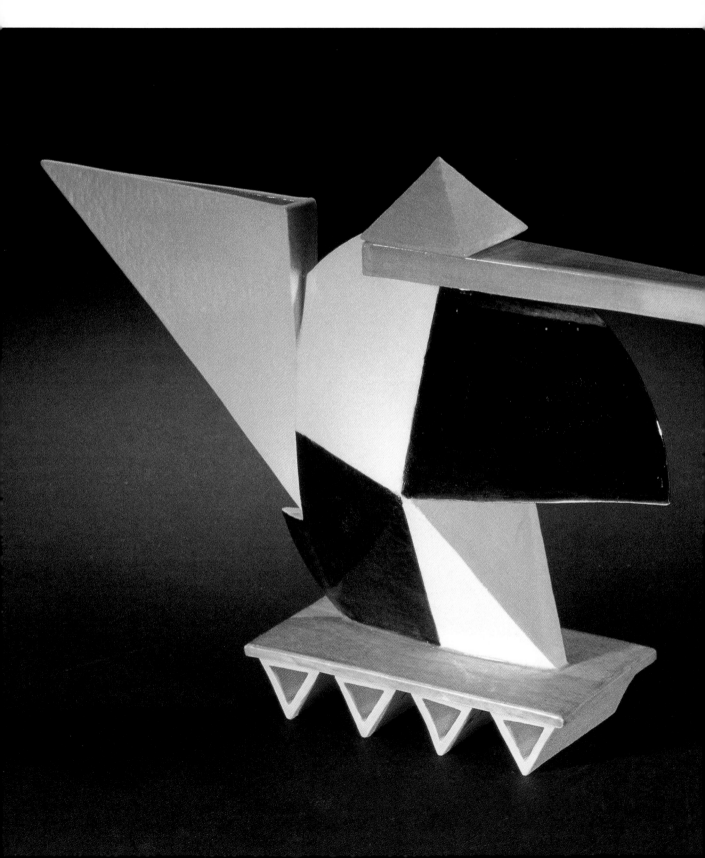

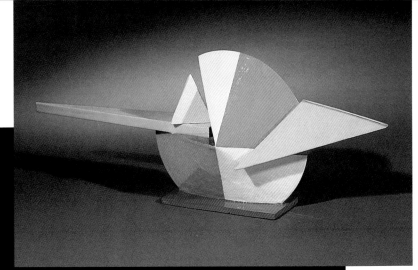

Left:
Pinwheel, 1980
12 in. high

Top:
Pinwheel, 1980
7 in. high

Above:
Pinwheel, 1980
12 × 18½ × 3¼ in.

Following pages:
Left:
Cactus, 1980
16 in. high

Right:
Trojan Parallelogram,
1981
9 in. high

71

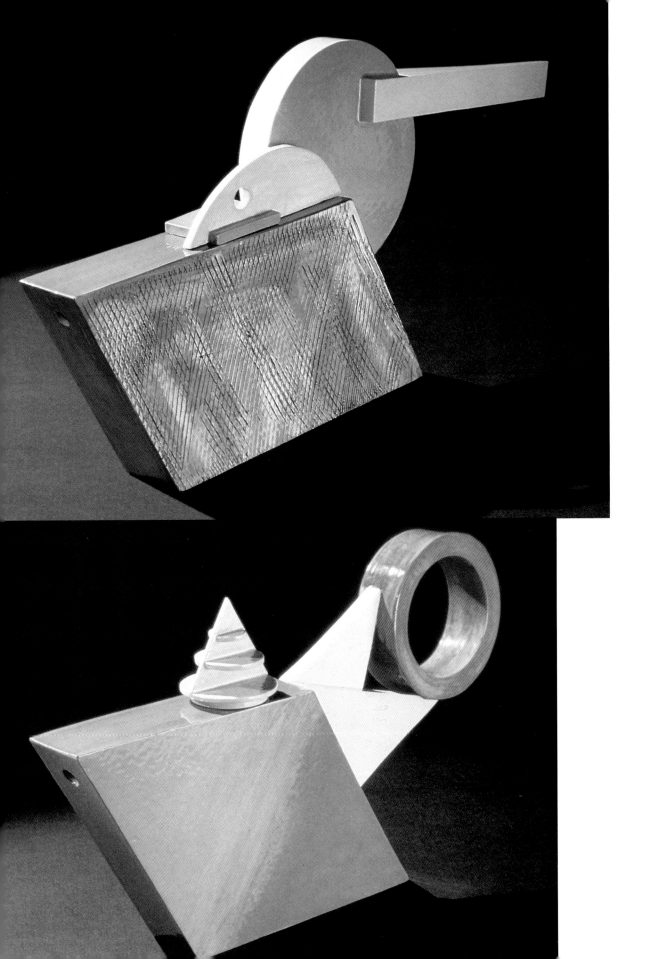

Preceding pages:
Top left:
Parallelogram, 1981
7¾ in. high

Bottom left:
Parallelogram, 1981
9 in. high

Top right:
Morley in Motion, 1981
12 in. high

Bottom right:
Parallelogram/Clothespin
Handle, 1981
9 in. high

Opposite:
Sengai, 1981
14 in. high

Above:
Sengai, 1981
14 in. high

Above:
Tea Types, 1981
14 in. high

Right:
Tea Types Teapot, 1981
14 in. high

Following pages:
Top left:
Two-Tone Cone, 1981
7½ in. high

Bottom left:
Cone, 1981
7½ in. high

Top right:
Scorpion Teapot, 1981
12½ in. high

Bottom right:
Two-Tone Cone, 1981
8 in. high

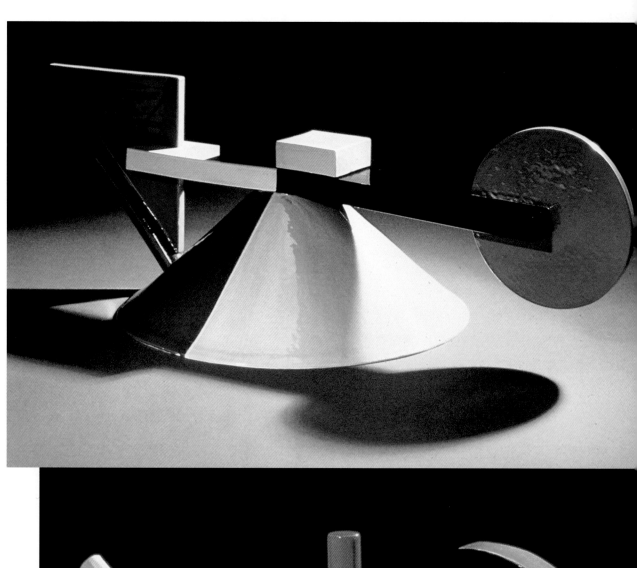

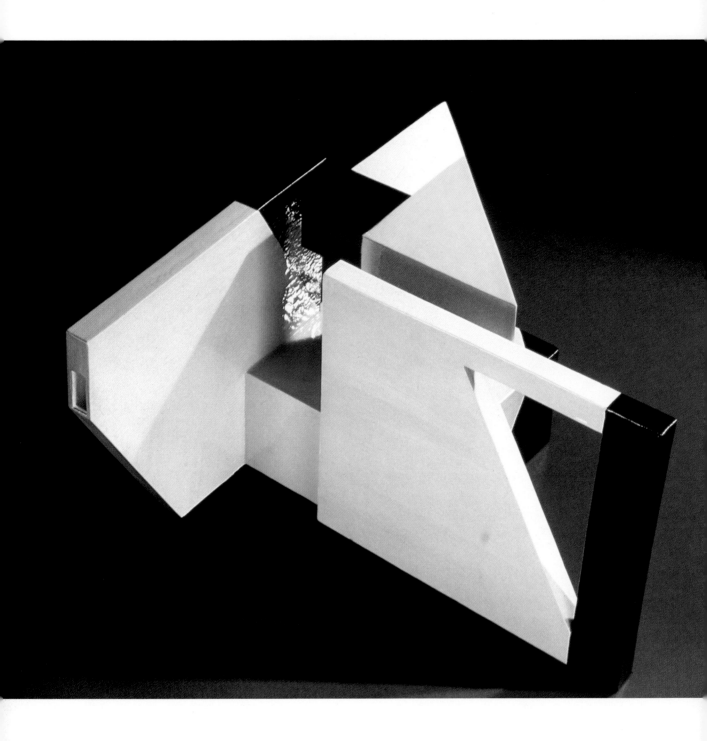

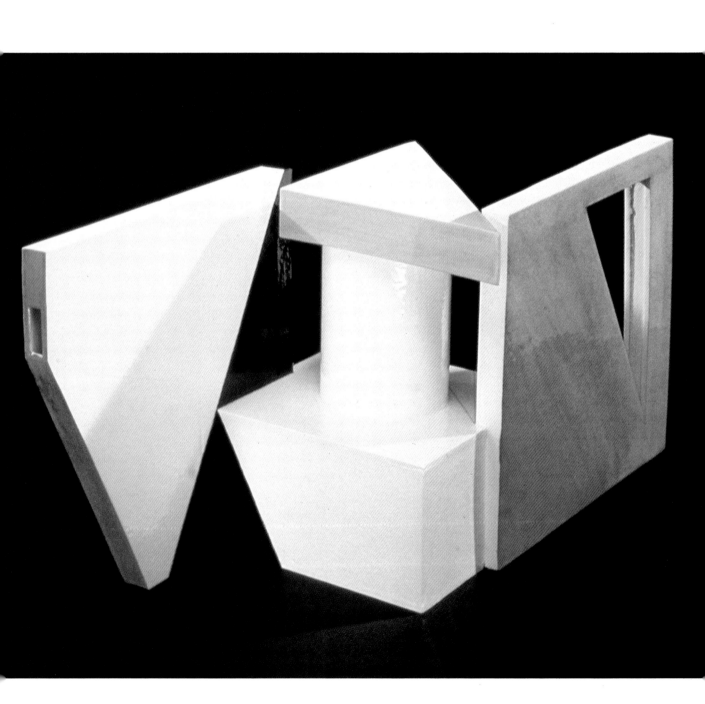

Previous pages:
Left:
Mexican Bauhaus, 1981
9 in. high

Right:
Mexican Bauhaus, 1981
9 in. high

Right:
Mexican Bauhaus
Extraordinaire, 1982
18 in. high

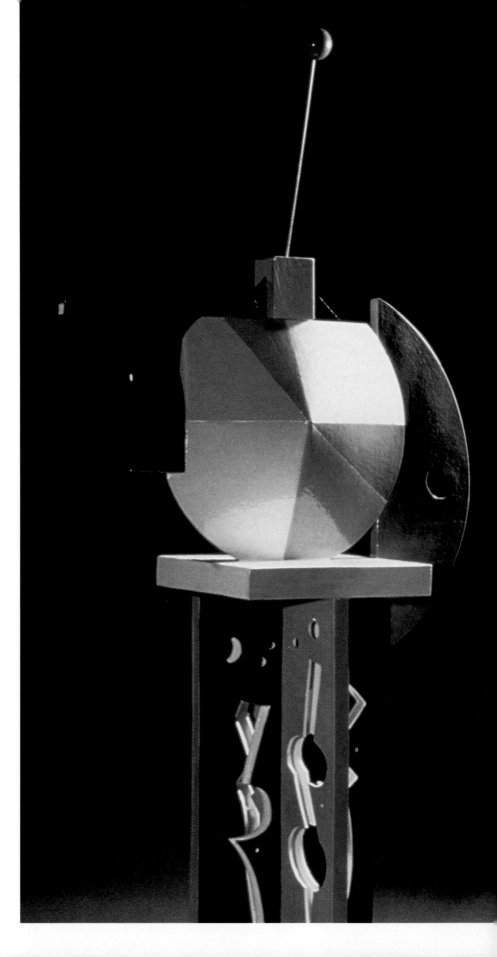

Right:
Towering Teatypes, 1981
38 × 18 × 10 in. high

Opposite:
Towering Teatypes, 1981
38 × 18 × 10 in.

Following pages:
Top left:
Parallelogram, 1981
10 in. high

Bottom left:
Parallelogram, 1981
10 in. high

Top right:
Parallelogram, 1981
12 in. high

Bottom right:
Parallelogram Eclipse,
1981
9½ in. high

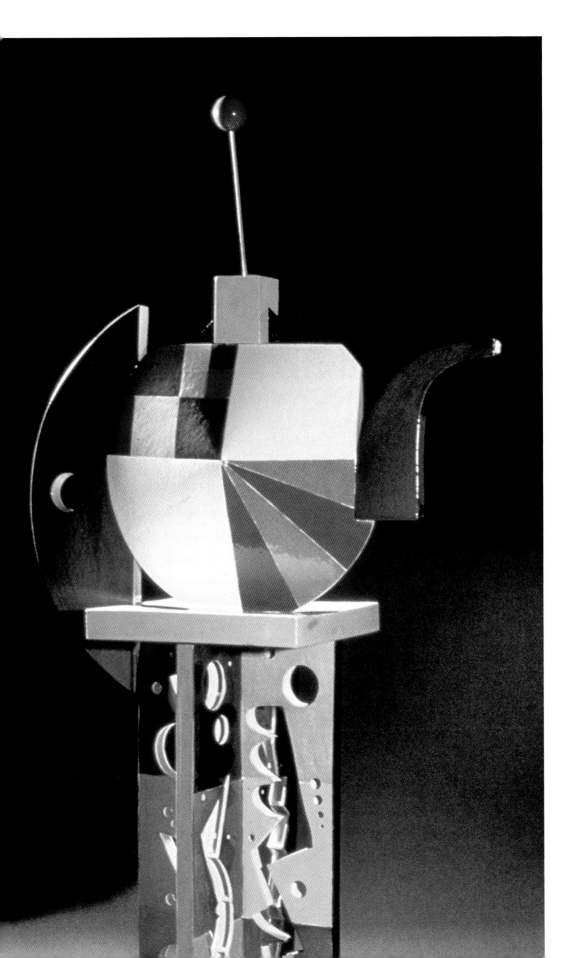

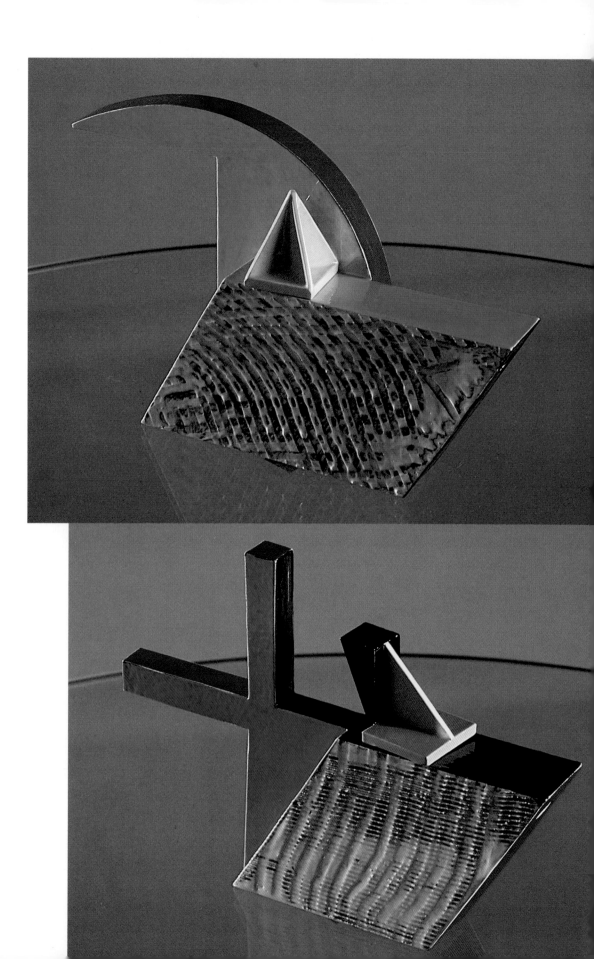

Preceding pages:
Left:
Rebar Series, 1981
16½ in. high

Right:
Tower Rebar, 1981
15 in. high

Above:
Mexican Bauhaus
Abridged, 1981
13 in. high

Right:
Mexican Bauhaus Sewer
Drainer, 1981
12 in. high

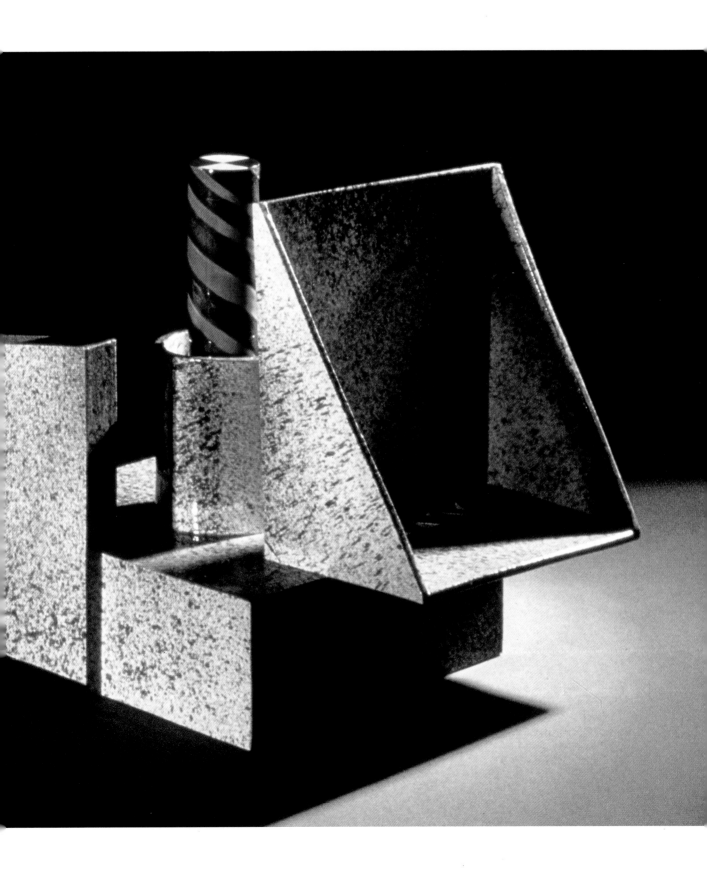

Left:
Weathervane, 1982
15½ × 24 × 10 in.

Top:
Weathervane, 1982
10½ in. high

Above:
Study for Weathervane,
1982
Ink on paper
14 × 20 in.

Following pages:
Left:
Accordion Series, 1984
18 × 18 × 6 in.

Right:
California Accordion,
1983
17 × 7 × 21 in.

95

MED GRAY

REG PURP OR BLUE GRAY

BLK

lite Yellow glaze

ICE BLUE SALMON

1

CAB YERL

LITE BLUE

DR GRAY

ALL GLAZE L TAPE

LITE BLUE OR GLAZE A1'GE

REG PURP.

YELLOW LAMIC BLACK WHITE

MED GREEN ETC

BLK

BLUE

PURPLE

16"

B

G

W

ETC

CRIM OR RUDY WARDS TURD

3

DOTS

ORI REL PURR

DR GR.

BRIGHT GREEN

ELECE BLUE EB

YELL

EB

CRIM RED

BLK EDGE.

MED GR.--C. WHITE

2

PINK

RED

PURP.

GRAY

BLK

OTTO CR

SE W

OTTO IRON

4

ORANGE

PURPS

PINK CRIM

CAD ORANGE

CAD GREEN

LITE BLUE

YELLOW

2

1

3

GREENS

GRAM WHITE GREEN

BLIL ETC

5

SEA TO DR.

IRD

DR GRAY

W

G

BL GR OR

WHITE

LITE PDUVA OR

SEA N PHG

BLUE PAINT

YELLOW

6

DOTS

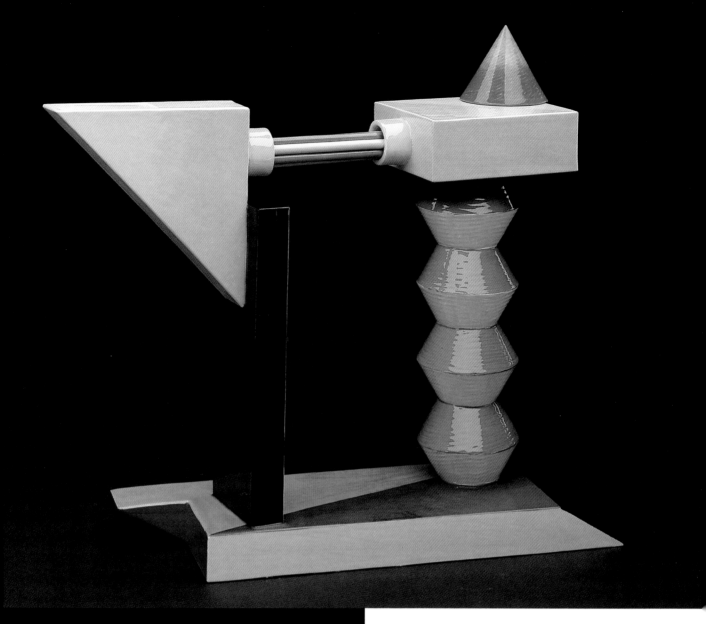

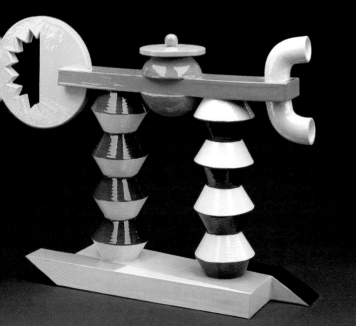

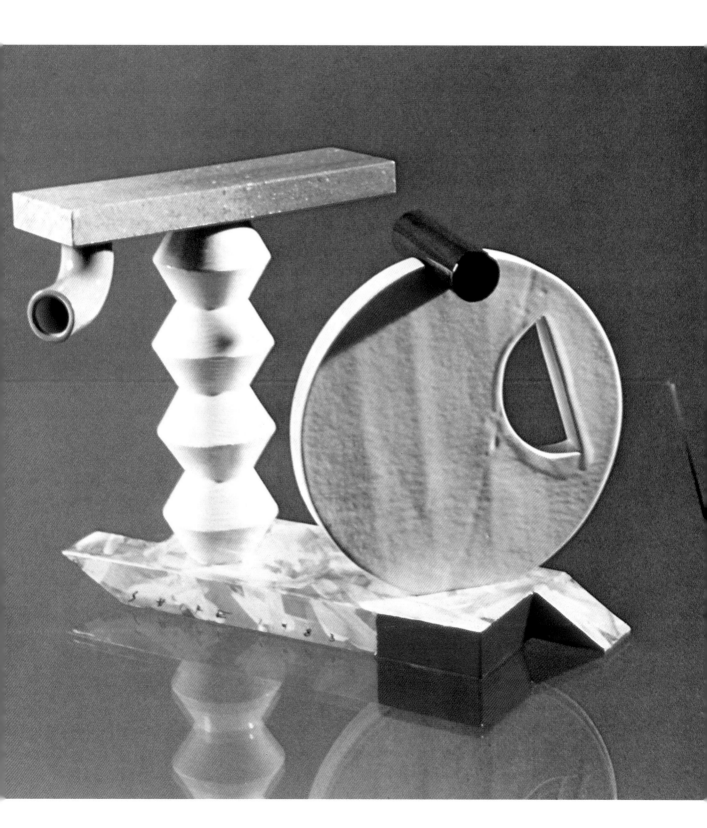

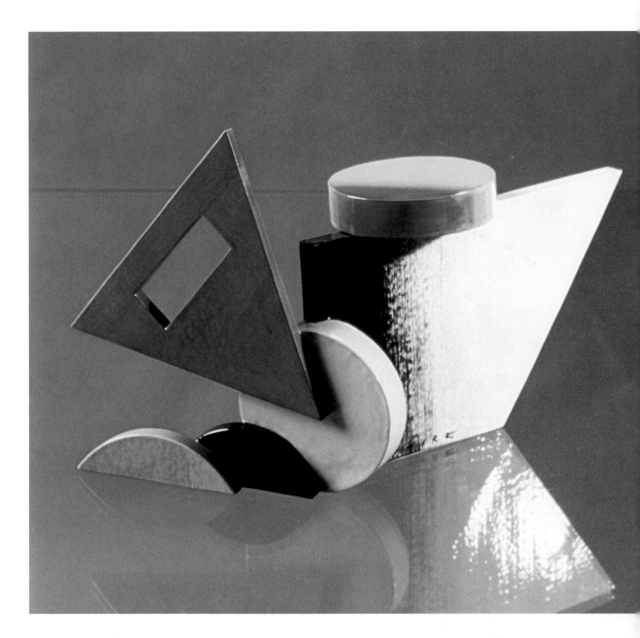

Above:
Third Man with 2 Lemon Slices, 1983
$11\frac{3}{4} \times 12 \times 8$ in.

Opposite:
Mexican Bauhaus, 1983
$14\frac{1}{2} \times 11 \times 12$ in.

Right:
Mexican Bauhaus
Olympic, 1983
11 × 9 × 17 in.

Following pages
Left:
Third Man, 1983
13 in. high

Right:
The Crank, 1983
18 × 18½ × 13½ in.

Opposite:
Thirdman Teapot, 1983
14 in. high

Above:
Viennese Wedge, 1984
9½ in. high

Above:
Scorpion Float, 1983
11½ in. high

Opposite
Scorpion Float, 1983
11½ in. high

Following pages:
Weathervane, 1983
12 in. high

Above:
Third Man, 1983
11 in. high

Right:
Third Man, 1983
14 in. high

Opposite:
Third Man, 1984
14 in. high

Above:
Viennese Wedge, 1983
23 × 18 × 7½ in.

Right:
Viennese Wedge, 1983
11½ × 14½ × 8 in.

Opposite:
Mexican Bauhaus Derrick
Funnel, 1983
10⅞ × 12½ × 10½ in.

Above:
<u>Mexican Bauhaus Can
Opener</u>, 1983
12 in. high

Opposite:
<u>Mexican Bauhaus Can
Opener</u>, 1983
10 in. high

Right:
Trellis, 1984
$11 \times 28 \times 16$ in.

Following pages:
Top left:
Spiral Trellis, 1984-85
11 in. high

Bottom left:
Spiral Trellis, 1984-85
11 in. high

Top right:
Trellis, 1984
$10 \times 18\frac{1}{8} \times 6$ in.

Bottom right:
Trellis, 1984
11 in. high

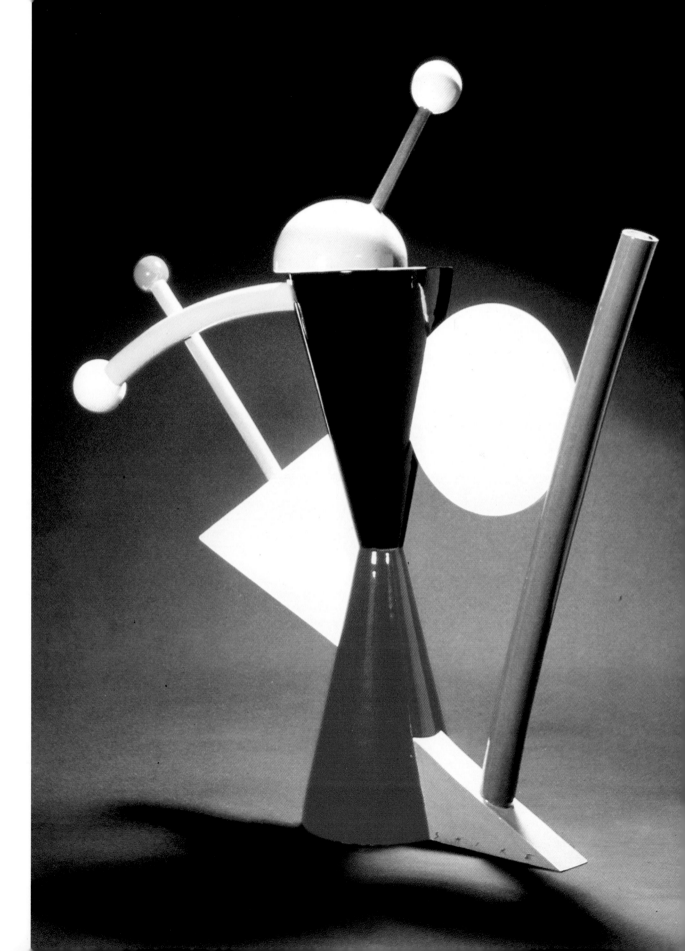

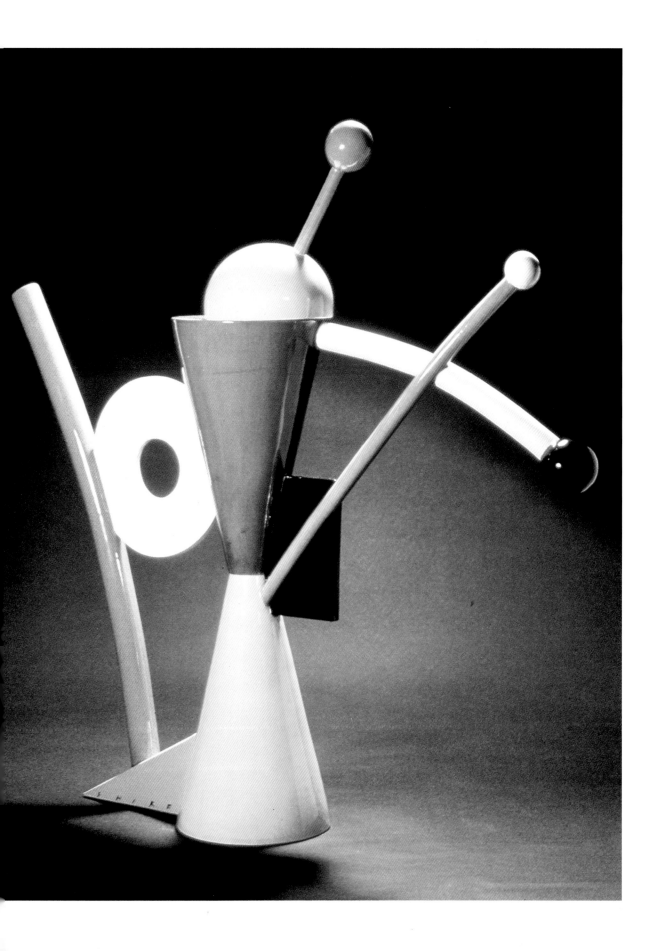

Preceding pages:
Left:
Hourglass Cloud
Chamber, 1984
24 in. high

Right:
Hourglass Cloud
Chamber, 1984
25 in. high

Above:
Hourglass, 1984
$24 \times 19\frac{1}{2} \times 5\frac{1}{2}$ in.

Right:
Son of Hourglass,
1984
24 in. high

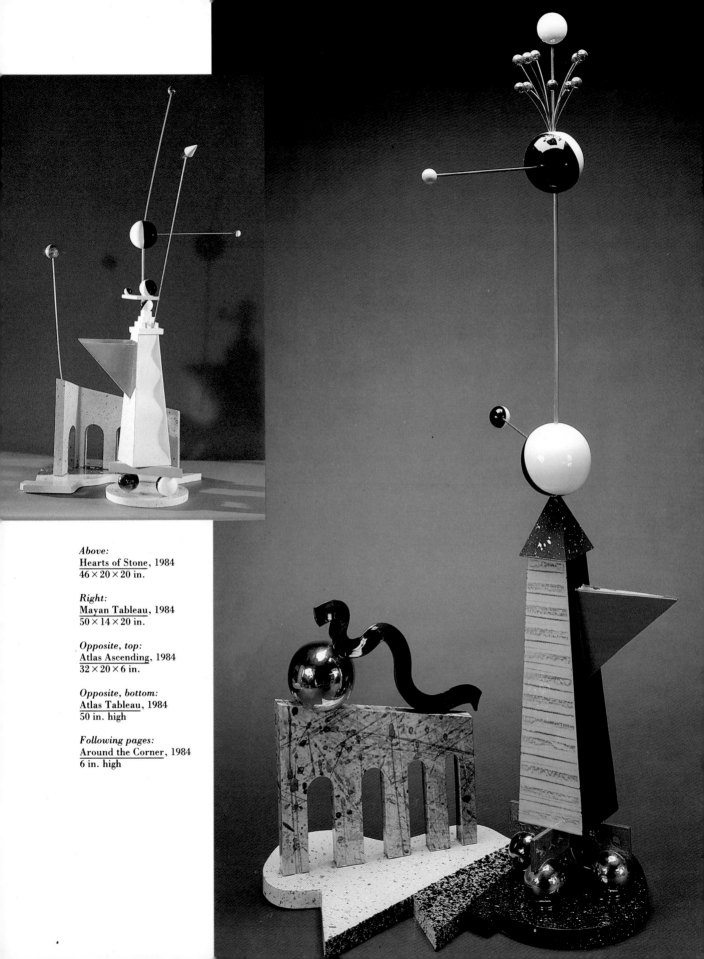

Above:
Hearts of Stone, 1984
$46 \times 20 \times 20$ in.

Right:
Mayan Tableau, 1984
$50 \times 14 \times 20$ in.

Opposite, top:
Atlas Ascending, 1984
$32 \times 20 \times 6$ in.

Opposite, bottom:
Atlas Tableau, 1984
50 in. high

Following pages:
Around the Corner, 1984
6 in. high

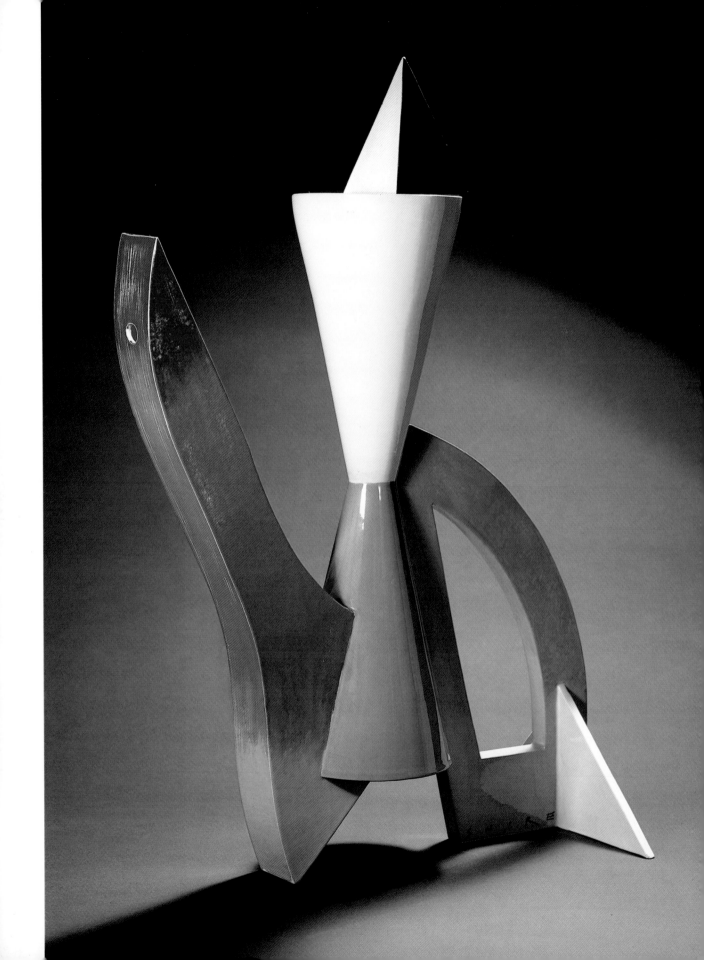

Opposite:
Hourglass, 1984
$25\frac{1}{2} \times 17\frac{1}{4} \times 6\frac{5}{8}$ in.

Left:
Baby Hourglass, 1984
$11\frac{1}{2}$ in. high

Above:
Peach Teapot, 1985
Gouache on paper
8 × 10 in.

Right:
T-Pot Study, 1982
Gouache on paper
10 × 14 in.

Opposite:
Chair for Combing Hair,
1985
Gouache on paper
9 × 14 in.

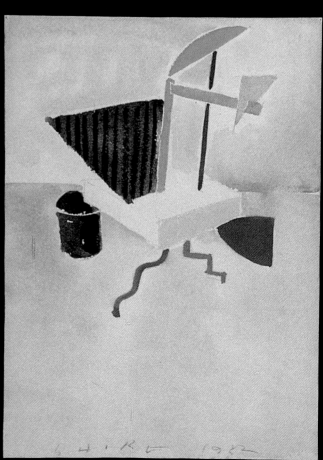

SHIRE 1985

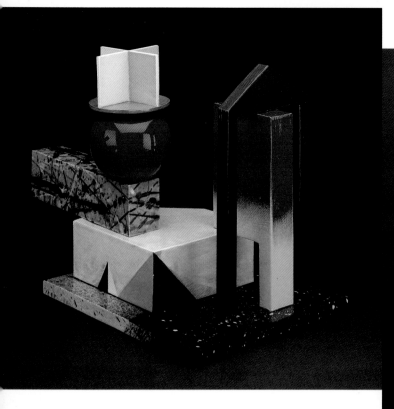

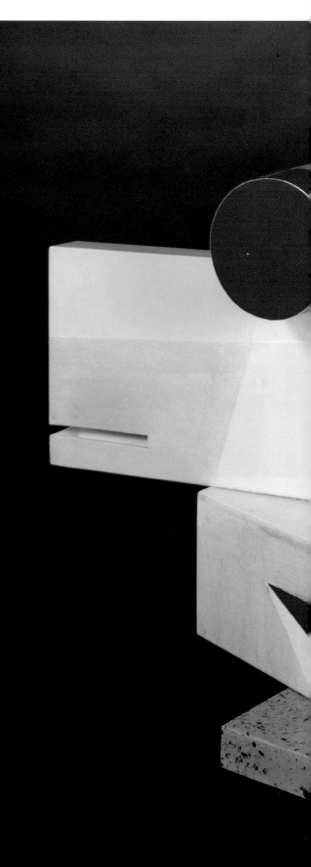

Above:
Dog Hedge, 1984
12 in. high

Right:
Large Dog Hedge, 1984
16 × 30 × 16 in.

Following pages:
Left:
Baby Hourglass, 1985
11 in. high

Right:
Baby Hourglass, 1984
10 in. high

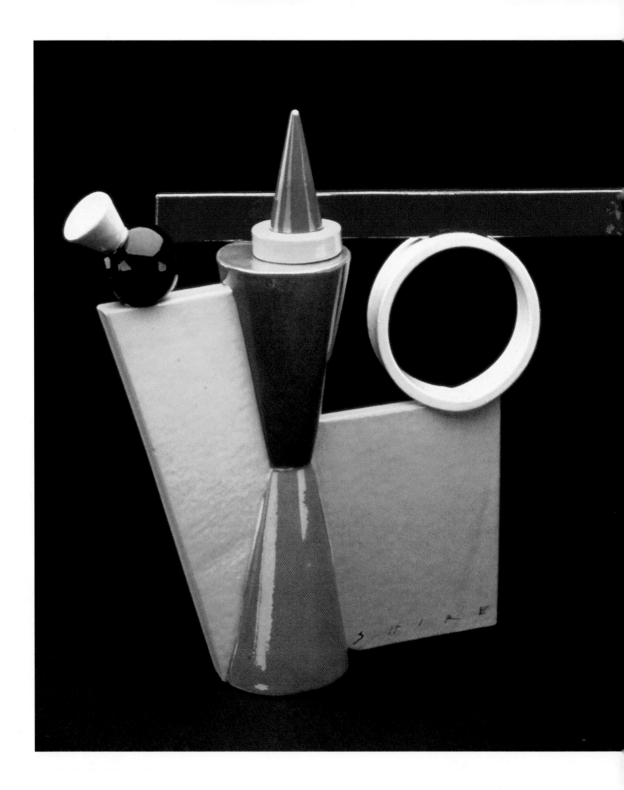

Top:
Dog Hedge Cove, 1984-85
11 in. high

Above:
Dog Hedge Cove, 1984-85
11 in. high

Right:
Dog Hedge Cove, 1983–84
10¼ × 16 × 14 in.

Right:
Dog Hedge Screaming
Picasso, 1985
10¼ in. high

Bibliography

Books:

Domergue, Denise. *Artists Design Furniture*. New York: Harry. N. Abrams, 1984.

Radice, Barbara. *Jewelry by Architects*. Milan: Electa. 1987; New York: Rizzoli International Publications, 1987.

Radice, Barbara. *Memphis*. Milan: Electa, 1984; New York: Rizzoli International Publications, 1984.

Shire, Peter. *Tea Types*. Los Angeles: Tea Garden Press, 1980.

Street-Porter, Tim. *Freestyle*. New York: Stewart, Tabori & Chang, 1986.

Magazines:

Book, Jeff. "Shades of Shire, A House of a Different Color in Echo Park." *Angeles*, December 1990.

Clothier, Peter. "A Carnival World of Color." *American Ceramics*, Spring 1989: 26-33.

Des Champs, Madeleine. "Designer du Precaire." *Modes*, France. January 1989: 25-31.

Glass, Judith. Review. *Art Week*, May 1975: 1.

Graf, Vera. "Die Neue Just am Design, Californien." *Architektur und Wohnen*, January 1987: 90-93.

Huneven, Michelle, "Shire Heaven." *California*, June 1989: 70-75, 132-134.

Janjigian, Robert. "From L.A. to Memphis." *Interiors*, October 1983: 72.

Nelson, Keiko. "Peter Shire, Colorful Magician Leading the World." "California Artist: Color and Works." *F.P.*, March 1988: 28-37.

Perrin, Deborah. "Mexican Bauhaus." *Arts and Architecture*, August 1982: 59-60.

Porges, Maria. "Peter Shire: Freeway." *American Craft*, December 1988: 50-55, 69.

Radice, Barbara. "Arte, Le Tiere di un Alice Cubista." *Modo*, July 1980: 56-57.

Rickey, Carrie. "Art Attack." *Art in America*, May 1981: 44-45.

Sykes, Gini. "What Inspires Shire." *Metropolis*, October 1985: 25.

Thun, Matteo. "Oggetto Californiano, Le Tiere di Peter Shire." *Casa Vogue*, May 1980: 230-231.

Wissinger, Joanna. "Peter Shire House, Los Angeles, California, Artful Craft." *Progressive Architecture*, September 1986: 107-109.

Illustration Credits